Influential Presidents
George Washington

by Emma Huddleston

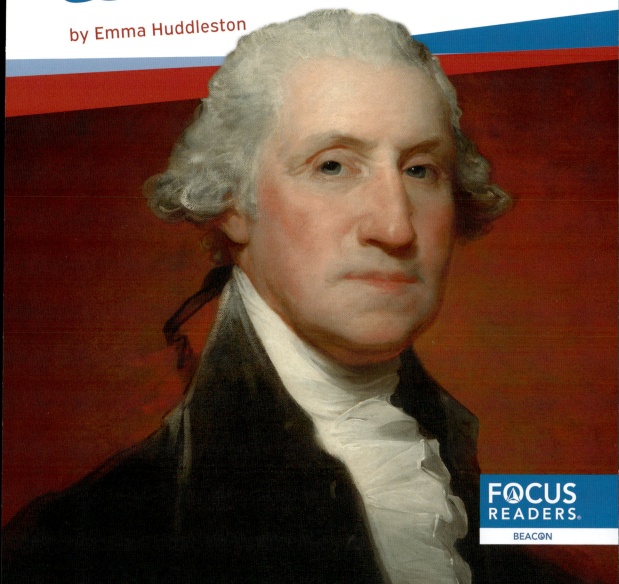

www.focusreaders.com

Copyright © 2023 by Focus Readers®, Lake Elmo, MN 55042. All rights reserved. No part of this book may be reproduced or utilized in any form or by any means without written permission from the publisher.

Focus Readers is distributed by North Star Editions:
sales@northstareditions.com | 888-417-0195

Produced for Focus Readers by Red Line Editorial.

Photographs ©: Shutterstock Images, cover, 1, 11, 14, 22, 27; North Wind Picture Archives/Alamy, 4; Everett Collection/Newscom, 7, 8; iStockphoto, 13, 29, 20–21; Ian Dagnall/Alamy, 16; Science History Images/Alamy, 19, 25

Library of Congress Cataloging-in-Publication Data
Names: Huddleston, Emma, author.
Title: George Washington / Emma Huddleston.
Description: Lake Elmo, MN : Focus Readers, [2023] | Series: Influential
  presidents | Includes bibliographical references and index. | Audience:
  Grades 2-3
Identifiers: LCCN 2022025513 (print) | LCCN 2022025514 (ebook) | ISBN
  9781637394687 (hardcover) | ISBN 9781637395059 (paperback) | ISBN
  9781637395769 (ebook pdf) | ISBN 9781637395424 (hosted ebook)
Subjects: LCSH: Washington, George, 1732-1799--Juvenile literature. |
  Presidents--United States--Biography--Juvenile literature. | United
  States--Politics and government--1775-1783--Juvenile literature. |
  United States--Politics and government--1783-1809--Juvenile literature.
Classification: LCC E312.66 .H84 2023 (print) | LCC E312.66 (ebook) | DDC
  973.4/1092 [B]--dc23/eng/20220527
LC record available at https://lccn.loc.gov/2022025513
LC ebook record available at https://lccn.loc.gov/2022025514

Printed in the United States of America
Mankato, MN
012023

About the Author

Emma Huddleston lives in Minnesota with her husband and daughter. She enjoys reading, writing, and staying active. She thinks learning about presidents is an important part of understanding how the United States works today.

Table of Contents

CHAPTER 1
The First President 5

CHAPTER 2
Military Leader 9

CHAPTER 3
A New Country 15

ISSUE SPOTLIGHT
Staying Neutral 20

CHAPTER 4
A Strong Example 23

Focus on George Washington • 28
Glossary • 30
To Learn More • 31
Index • 32

Chapter 1

The First President

George Washington felt nervous. He stood in front of a big crowd. The date was April 30, 1789. Washington was about to become the first US president. He got ready to take an **oath**.

George Washington took his oath at Federal Hall in New York City.

First, he placed his hand on a Bible. Next, he promised to protect the country's laws. Washington's hands shook as he spoke. He was anxious about being president. No one had ever held this job before. He did not have any examples to guide him.

Today, presidents take their oaths in Washington, DC. But in 1789, that city had not been built yet.

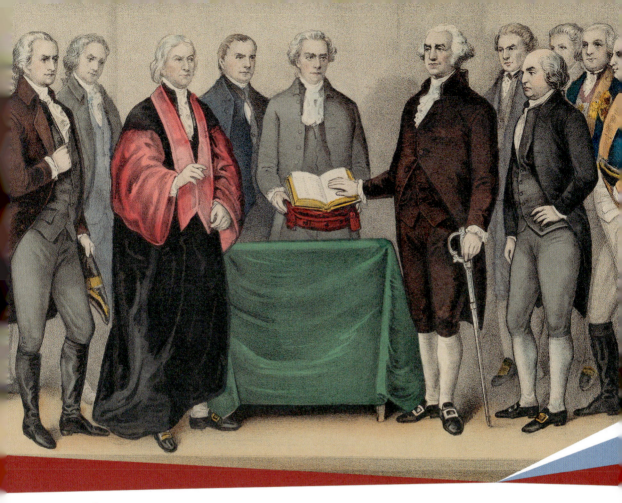

 New York City was the US capital when Washington took his oath.

Washington knew that others would study what he did. He hoped to set a good example. He wanted to be a fair and careful leader.

Chapter 2

Military Leader

George Washington was born on February 22, 1732. He grew up in Virginia. It was a British **colony**. George's father owned a farm. He held people of African descent in slavery. He forced them to work.

George Washington was born at Popes Creek Plantation in Virginia.

When George was 11, his father died. As a result, George now held the slaves. He held many more slaves when he was an adult.

Washington joined the military when he was 20. He became a leader. He fought for the British.

Did You Know?

Washington fought in the French and Indian War (1754–1763). This war was between the British and the French. Both sides wanted to control parts of North America.

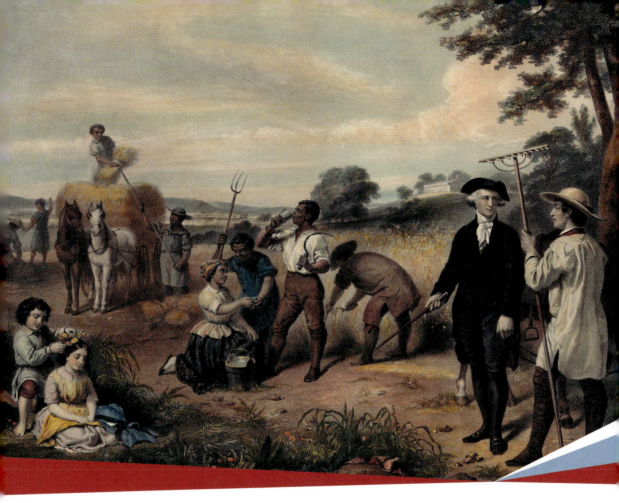

 Washington held hundreds of people in slavery during his lifetime.

Over time, Washington started to think British rule was unfair. Other people agreed. In 1775, the colonies fought against the British.

It was the start of the Revolutionary War (1775–1783).

Washington led the colonies' army. His troops were poorly trained. They had little food. They had few supplies. But Washington kept his troops focused. He told them not to give up.

Did You Know?

When the Revolutionary War first started, colonists were not fighting for **independence**. They did not call for independence until 1776.

 Washington leads his soldiers during the winter of 1776.

Washington led his army to victory. The United States became independent. Washington was a national hero.

13

Chapter 3

A New Country

After the war, the United States was a new country. It needed laws. It had to create a government. This process was difficult. The first laws did not work well. The government was too weak. It had no leader.

Washington returned to his home at Mount Vernon when the war ended.

 Washington takes part in the signing of the US Constitution.

In 1787, lawmakers decided to start over. George Washington led a group that wrote the **Constitution**. This set of laws created a stronger government. It also created a new job. A president would lead the country. This person would make sure people followed the laws.

Washington hoped to go back to his farm. He wanted to spend time with his family. But many people wanted him to be president. Washington answered their call. In 1789, he became the first president of the United States.

In the 1789 election, Washington won all the votes. Nobody ran against him.

Washington chose four people for his cabinet. This group advised the president. They helped him make hard decisions. Washington also created a new capital for the United States. This city later became known as Washington, DC.

Did You Know?

Today's presidents have larger cabinets than Washington did. For example, President Joe Biden had more than 20 people in his cabinet.

 The people in Washington's cabinet often disagreed with one another.

Washington also chose the first members of the Supreme Court. Their job was to decide legal cases. Washington played a large role in forming the new government.

19

ISSUE SPOTLIGHT

Staying Neutral

In the 1790s, the British and French were at war. Many people asked Washington to help one side or the other. But Washington believed the best idea was to stay **neutral**.

The United States did not join the war. Washington wanted to give the country a chance to develop. Being neutral meant the United States did not have to spend time and money on a war. Instead, the country could use that time and money to improve itself.

Both the French and British wanted help from the United States to win the French Revolutionary Wars.

Chapter 4

A Strong Example

George Washington would have been happy to serve only one **term**. But people wanted him to serve a second term. Washington agreed to do it. He worked to be a leader for all parts of the country.

Washington arrives at Congress Hall in Philadelphia to take the oath for his second term.

Washington traveled through states in the north. He traveled through states in the south, too. He listened to people with different ideas.

In his second term, Washington signed **treaties** with other countries. These agreements helped the United States trade with Great Britain and Spain.

Many people asked Washington to serve a third term. But he said no. He was tired of his job.

 In 1794, Washington helped stop a violent protest against taxes.

In 1796, Washington gave a final message. He told people to stay **united**. He warned against **political parties**. He worried that these groups would divide people.

Washington also said that future leaders should stay out of other countries' problems.

Washington went back to his home in Virginia. He spent only two years there. On December 14, 1799, he died.

Washington set a strong example for future presidents. He helped

Did You Know?

The state of Washington is named after the first president.

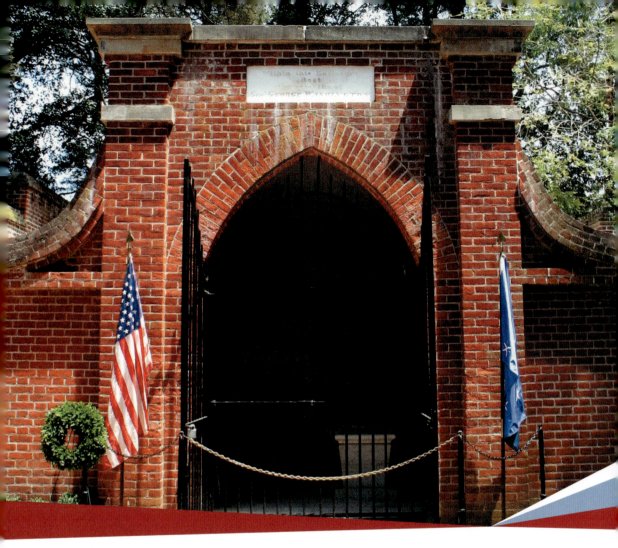

 George Washington and his wife, Martha, are buried outside their home in Mount Vernon.

set up the country's government. He also encouraged people with different beliefs to work together.

27

FOCUS ON

George Washington

Write your answers on a separate piece of paper.

1. Write a paragraph that explains the main ideas of Chapter 3.

2. Do you agree with Washington's advice to stay neutral? Why or why not?

3. When did Washington become president?
   - **A.** 1776
   - **B.** 1789
   - **C.** 1799

4. Why did Washington become a national hero?
   - **A.** He led his troops to victory over the British.
   - **B.** He decided not to serve a third term.
   - **C.** He warned against political parties.

5. What does **anxious** mean in this book?

Washington's hands shook as he spoke. He was anxious about being president.

    A. feeling strong
    B. feeling tired
    C. feeling worried

6. What does **advised** mean in this book?

Washington chose four people for his cabinet. This group advised the president. They helped him make hard decisions.

    A. chose a new president
    B. helped someone decide
    C. became a country's leader

Answer key on page 32.

Glossary

colony
An area controlled by a country that is far away.

Constitution
The document that lays out the basic beliefs and laws of the United States.

independence
The ability to make decisions without being controlled by another government.

neutral
Not supporting either side in a disagreement.

oath
A serious promise to behave in a certain way.

political parties
Groups that have specific ideas about how the government should be run.

term
The amount of time a person can serve after being elected.

treaties
Official agreements that are made between two or more countries or groups.

united
Working toward the same goal.

To Learn More

BOOKS

Britton, Tamara L. *George Washington*. Minneapolis: Abdo Publishing, 2021.

Murray, Laura K. *George Washington*. North Mankato, MN: Capstone Press, 2020.

Regan, Michael. *George Washington and the American Presidency*. Lake Elmo, MN: Focus Readers, 2018.

NOTE TO EDUCATORS

Visit **www.focusreaders.com** to find lesson plans, activities, links, and other resources related to this title.

Index

C
cabinet, 18
colonies, 9, 11–12
Constitution, 16

F
France, 10, 20
French and Indian War, 10

G
Great Britain, 9–11, 20, 24

N
neutrality, 20
North America, 10

O
oath, 5–6

R
Revolutionary War, 12, 20

S
slavery, 9–10
Supreme Court, 19

T
treaties, 24

V
Virginia, 9, 26

W
Washington, DC, 6, 18

Answer Key: 1. Answers will vary; **2.** Answers will vary; **3.** B; **4.** A; **5.** C; **6.** B